First Look: Science

A Seed in Need

A First Look at the Plant Cycle

by Sam Godwin **illustrated by Simone Abel**

Thanks to our reading adviser:

Susan Kesselring, M.A., Literacy Educator
Rosemount-Apple Valley-Eagan (Minnesota) School District

PICTURE WINDOW BOOKS
Minneapolis, Minnesota

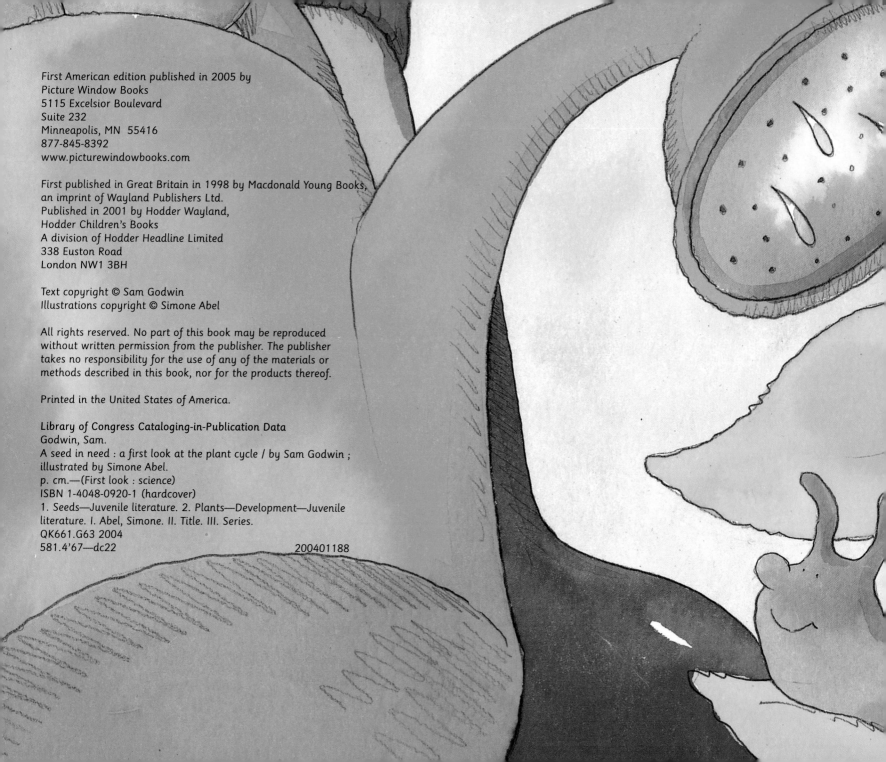

First American edition published in 2005 by
Picture Window Books
5115 Excelsior Boulevard
Suite 232
Minneapolis, MN 55416
877-845-8392
www.picturewindowbooks.com

First published in Great Britain in 1998 by Macdonald Young Books,
an imprint of Wayland Publishers Ltd.
Published in 2001 by Hodder Wayland,
Hodder Children's Books
A division of Hodder Headline Limited
338 Euston Road
London NW1 3BH

Printed in the United States of America.

Library of Congress Cataloging-in-Publication Data
Godwin, Sam.
A seed in need : a first look at the plant cycle / by Sam Godwin ;
illustrated by Simone Abel.
p. cm.—(First look : science)
ISBN 1-4048-0920-1 (hardcover)
1. Seeds—Juvenile literature. 2. Plants—Development—Juvenile
literature. I. Abel, Simone. II. Title. III. Series.
QK661.G63 2004
581.4'67—dc22   200401188

For all the seedlings at Burgess Hill School – SG

With love to Chris, Chloe, and Grace – SA

3

Deep in the ground lies a seed.

It's cold, and the seed is asleep.

Let me see. A seed needs air, water, and warmth to make it grow. Seeds cannot grow when it's very cold.

5

That's right.

The sun warms the soil, and the seed wakes up.

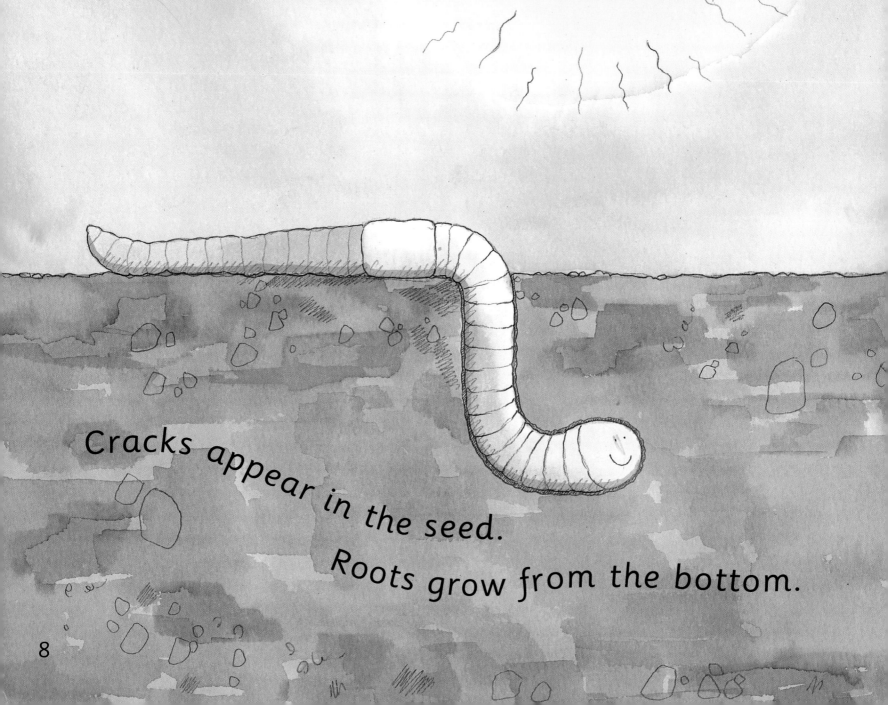

Cracks appear in the seed.
Roots grow from the bottom.

A small shoot grows from the seed.

Roots hold the plant firmly in the soil. They soak up water, too.

9

The white shoot pushes its way through the soil.

10

The seedling turns greener. Its stem grows thicker

and stronger, and leaves appear on it.

How do plants get food?

Leaves use sunlight to make food for the plant.

Children water the plant and give it extra food.

14

It grows taller and thicker and bushier.

When the weather is dry, plants need to be watered.

15

It's May, and the garden is full of creatures

who seek shelter under the plant's leaves.

A bud appears on the plant. At first, it is small

The bud turns into a beautiful flower.

Bees and butterflies come to visit.

Look at the insects coming to drink nectar from the flower.

Summer is over, and the flower begins to droop.
The petals fall to the ground.

23

The gardener carefully collects the seeds from

the center of the dead flower and stores them in a box.

Not all seeds are collected by gardeners. Some seeds just fall to the ground and grow on their own next spring.

Next spring, he will plant them in the soil again.

The Sunflower

Insects carry pollen dust from one flower to another on their legs and wings.

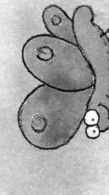

Petals are the colorful parts around the middle of a flower.

Pollen is the yellow dust found in the middle of a flower.

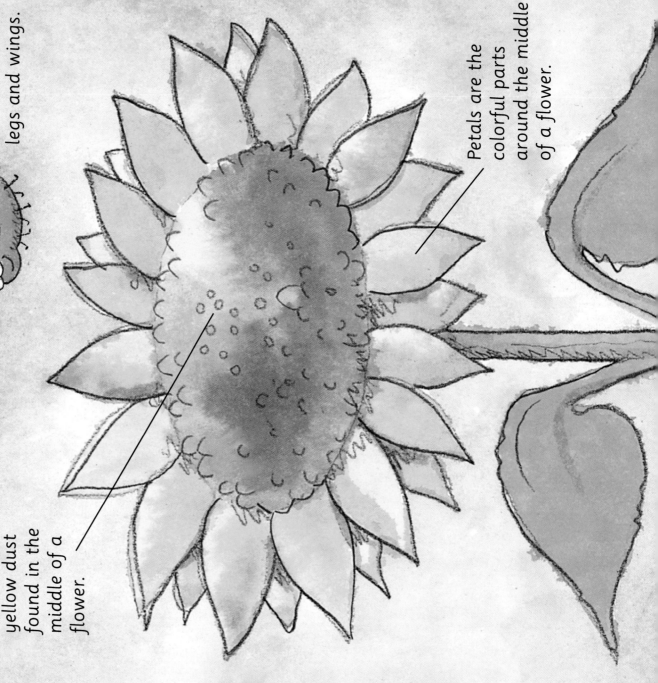

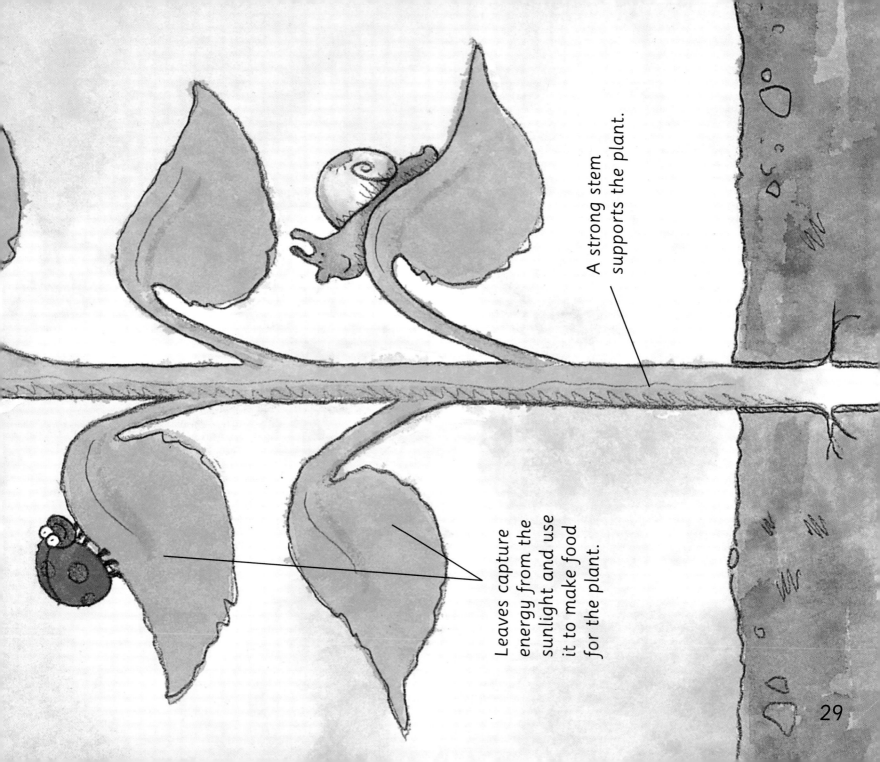

A strong stem supports the plant.

Leaves capture energy from the sunlight and use it to make food for the plant.

29

Useful Words

Bud
A flower that hasn't opened yet.

Nectar
A sweet juice inside a flower that attracts bees and butterflies.

Pollen
Yellow dust that helps plants make new seeds.

Root
The underground part of a plant that sucks food and water from the soil. Roots also help keep a plant in place.

Seed
The small, hard part of a plant from which a new plant grows.

Seedling
A very young plant.

Shoot
The white stem growing out of a seed that becomes a plant.

Fun Facts

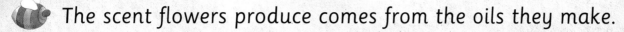 The scent flowers produce comes from the oils they make.

About 85 percent of the greenery on Earth is found in the oceans.

Not a single wild plant has a flower or blossom that is absolutely black.

The greens of a dandelion can be eaten. They help remove water from your body.

To Learn More

At the Library

Carle, Eric. *The Tiny Seed*. Saxonville, Mass.: Picture Book Studio, 1990.

Fowler, Allan. *From Seed to Plant*. New York: Children's Press, 2001.

Jordan, Helene J. *How a Seed Grows*. New York: HarperCollins, 1992.

On the Web

FactHound offers a safe, fun way to find Web sites related to this book. All of the sites on FactHound have been researched by our staff.

1. Visit *www.facthound.com*
2. Type in this special code: 1404809201
3. Click the FETCH IT button.

Your trusty FactHound will fetch the best Web sites for you!

Index

Look for all the books in this series:

A Seed in Need
A First Look at the Plant Cycle

And Everyone Shouted, "Pull!"
A First Look at Forces of Motion

From Little Acorns ...
A First Look at the Life Cycle of a Tree

Paint a Sun in the Sky
A First Look at the Seasons

Take a Walk on a Rainbow
A First Look at Color

The Case of the Missing Caterpillar
A First Look at the Life Cycle of a Butterfly

The Drop Goes Plop
A First Look at the Water Cycle

The Hen Can't Help It
A First Look at the Life Cycle of a Chicken

The Trouble with Tadpoles
A First Look at the Life Cycle of a Frog